KWIAN AND THE LAZY SUN

|kua|kuatten sseg |ne !gweeten !uhi′ ssin hi !nwa.
The stars shall sail along upon their footprints.
| ||kabbo of the San

For Laura and Victoria
                    —M. L.

For Johsanna, my daughter, who lights my world.
                                        —C.R.

Kwian and the Lazy Sun is based on "The Children Are Sent to
Throw the Sleeping Sun into the Sky," as told by ||kabbo of the
San. This story is included in *Specimens of Bushman Folklore*,
collected by W. H. I. Bleek and L. C. Lloyd. London: George
Allen & Company, Ltd., 1911.

This story is from the San of South Africa.

Library of Congress Cataloging-in-Publication Data

Lilly, Melinda.
    Kwian and the lazy sun: African tales and myths / retold by Melinda Lilly;
illustrated by Charles Reasoner.
        p. cm.
    "A San myth."
    Summary: In order to have light, Kwian and the other children throw another
villager, the lazy Kattenttu, into the sky where he becomes the sun.
    ISBN 1-57103-243-6
    [1. San (African people)—Folklore. 2. Folklore—South Africa.]   I. Reasoner,
Charles, ill. II. Title
PZ8.1.L468Kw 1998
398.2'089'961—dc21   98–22311
                                                                              CIP
                                                                              AC

Printed in the USA

African Tales and Myths

KWIAN
AND THE LAZY SUN

A San Myth

Retold by
Melinda Lilly

Illustrated by
Charles Reasoner

The Rourke Press, Inc.
Vero Beach, Florida 32964

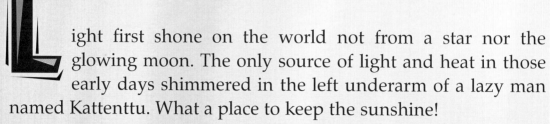

ight first shone on the world not from a star nor the glowing moon. The only source of light and heat in those early days shimmered in the left underarm of a lazy man named Kattenttu. What a place to keep the sunshine!

Kattenttu didn't exactly feel honored to be the light of the world. All day every day he'd stand on a mound of sand in the center of the village. He'd hold his skinny arm up, giving out light while the children played with their tzenee sticks, the women peeled roots for food, and the men sewed clothing from animal hides. The people took turns helping Kattenttu hold up his arm and even built a brace for it out of a gemsbok antelope horn and a tree branch, but he remained uncomfortable and tired.

Kattenttu's nights were not much easier for him than his days. As he rested on the sand, people warmed themselves by his nighttime flames. They sang and danced around the underarm campfire—bothering him when he was trying to sleep.

To entertain Kattenttu and help him stay awake, a keen-eyed girl named Kwian would tell him stories of the great desert beyond his light.

Like the Owl, Kwian's farseeing eyes could see as well in the dark as in the bright village. She would gaze past the straw huts and nearby hills. "In the Kalahari," she would say, "I can see springbok gazelles leaping over the grass like dancers. Cheetah whips through the shadowy landscape like a yellow wind. The air is heavy with darkness—"

"Darkness?" Kattenttu would interrupt. "Oh, to sleep in such darkness would be wonderful!"

When Kattenttu was awake, he daydreamed of sleep. One day right after breakfast he announced, "It's nighttime. Everybody sleep." He quickly lowered his arm, lay upon the sand, and slept. The village darkened with the colors of sunset.

Shaking their heads in confusion, the people met in the center of the village, a few steps away from where Kattenttu napped.

"I don't want to sleep!" exclaimed a small girl. "I just got up!"

"He gives us no time to collect the roots or cook the bulbs," complained a thin old woman.

"He won't help us hunt, says he's too tired," added a young father as he played with his baby son.

"Our days are too short and our evenings are too long," said a healer, tapping a small tortoise shell.

"Something must be done." All nodded their heads in agreement.

Kwian stood looking into the desert, searching for an answer to her peoples' problems. She knew the Kalahari hid its secrets in shadows that only she could find. "There has to be another light out there, beyond even what I can see," she said, gazing into the villagers' worried eyes. "I can make my way in the darkness. I will find a light." She picked up an ostrich eggshell filled with water and headed across the sand as her people sang songs of blessing and protection.

9

She walked silently in the Twilight Land, her eyes alert to any movement. In a cluster of shadowy trees, she came upon a family of prancing ostriches. "Great Ttoi," she called to them. "I am looking for light. My people need it to guide their way to water and food."

"Light? Child, can you see in the dark?" asked Father Ttoi Ostrich, ruffling his black and white feathers. "A sand flea is biting me. Pick it out, will you?"

Squinting, Kwian finally found the nit underneath Ostrich's wing and flicked it away.

"This way to light," said Father Ttoi Ostrich, heading to a water hole. He leaned over the pool of rainwater. "Light comes from this pond. See it all around that beautiful water bird?" Ttoi asked, not realizing he was admiring the reflections of the dimly lit sky and himself.

"Thank you, Father Ttoi," said Kwian, disappointed. She scanned the landscape, looking for a source of light, not its reflection. She spotted a herd of springbok gazelles nibbling grass and hurried toward them, hoping they could help her with her search.

"Graceful Whai," she called.

Too far to be able to see Kwian clearly, a small Whai Springbok tensed. "Hunter!" he cried. As one, the herd leaped into the air and scampered away to a cluster of bushes.

"I only hunt light," promised Kwian, slowly coming closer to the springboks.

"You have the eyes of a hunter," cautious Springbok said. "But now that you are near I can see you won't harm us. Perhaps you can help us, hunter of light. You see farther than we do. Tell us, are there hunters on the other side of the low hills?"

Kwian stared across the dark expanse, her sight traveling like a swift bird through the trees and over the hills. "There's no hunter of springbok—you'll be safe on the other side of the hills," she said. "There's a tall praying mantis striding this way, but that's all."

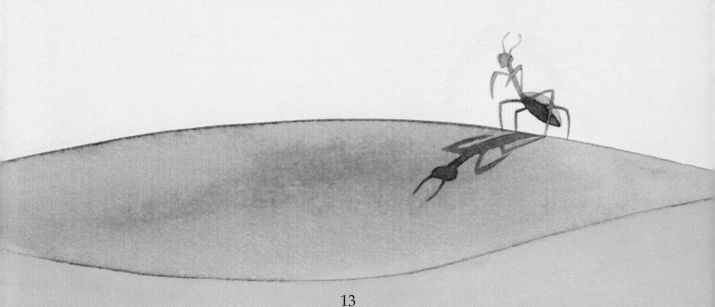

14

As she watched, Praying Mantis stopped walking. His feelers twitched in her direction and he stared back at her! Then he strode over the hills, his legs and arms like blades of grass blowing across the sand.

Kwian went toward him and looked up into a shiny face as silvery green as a pond of rain. "Greetings," said Praying Mantis in a singsong voice. "What are you doing in the shadow world, village girl?"

Kwian stared at the wondrous insect. "Looking for light," she answered, offering Mantis water from her eggshell. He sipped as she explained. "My people can't see to travel across the desert or make clothing. We have light from Kattenttu's underarm, but he only wants to curl up and rest. Do you know of another light?"

Mantis lifted his leather sandal and brushed sand off an ancient green foot. "Of course," he said. The green face creased into a grin. "I see light everywhere."

"Can you show me where it is?" Kwian asked, looking around her.

"No," replied Mantis, cocking his head and looking into her eyes. "Like you, I see many things. I know you saw in the dark for Ttoi Ostrich and you saw the distant sands for Whai Springbok. Now see light for your people."

18

Kwian searched the sky, the ground, the trees, a herd of eland antelope, a marabou stork—all was in shadow. She slowly turned around, her eyes seeking in each direction, seeing nothing. In frustration, she turned back to Mantis. He preened as she studied him. "How do you shine in this dim light?" she wondered aloud.

"Handsome, yes?" he asked, laughing.

Kwian focused on the horizon and looked at Mantis out of the corner of her eye. Something glimmered. "Your shoe," she said, pointing at it. "It gleams. That's why you are shiny."

"You found it!" Mantis grinned. "Congratulations, you can see in the light as well as in the dark!"

19

He scuffed his shoe in the pale sand. "Now, for those who can't see in the dark, let me get more dirt on my sandal. See if it will glow. See if it will walk." He suddenly jerked the shoe out of the sand, leaned back, and flung it upward. Kwian watched it flip in the air.

"Walk in the sky, Shoe!" laughed Mantis. "And become Moon!"

The shoe traveled across the heavens with shining footsteps. Then it tripped on the blackness and stuck against the sky. It was Moon. Light cascaded down from Shoe Moon like grains of sand.

Praying Mantis slung his other shoes over his shoulder and chuckled to himself as he walked away. Then he looked back at Kwian. "Help Kattenttu as we helped my shoe," he said. "Kattenttu is stuck in the wrong place."

Kwian raised her arm. "May you walk on beams of light," she said as Praying Mantis strolled across the glimmering landscape. Then she looked up at Shoe Moon and smiled. She now knew how to help her people and Kattenttu.

Heading for home she ran by Whai, the springboks lifting their heads as she raced past. She rushed past Ttoi, the family of ostriches still admiring their reflections in the water. She sprinted across the vast sand toward the village huts glowing in the moonlight.

As she arrived, the people danced to welcome her and celebrate Shoe Moon. Only Kattenttu slept. He snored on his mound of sand, his arms pressed to his sides as though trying to keep in the light.

When Moon sank out of the western sky Kwian whispered her plan to the other children. Then they tiptoed single file up to Kattenttu. A shaft of sunshine peeked from his underarm and bathed them with the colors of dawn.

Following Kwian's lead, the children gently slid their hands under Kattenttu. Lifting as one, they picked him up. He was as heavy as an eland antelope bull! They strained and struggled not to drop him.

His arm flopped away from his side and the flame from his underarm flared up! The fire spread throughout his body. He became hotter and hotter. He glowed orange yellow!

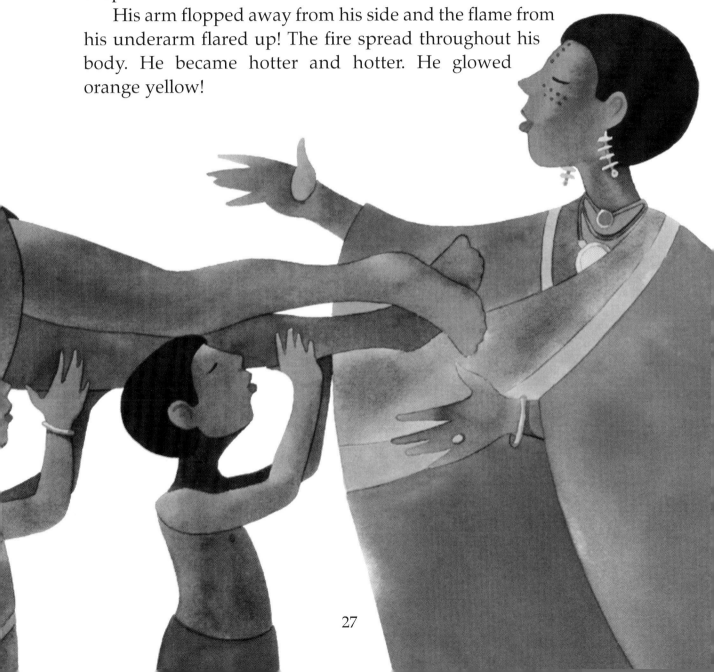

27

OW! The children's hands were burning! They jumped, flinging him up to the empty sky. Kattenttu shot across the blue like a flame. He stretched as he dreamed of the endless heavens. He yawned. Then he opened his eyes and nearly tumbled out of the sky in confusion! Where was he? What was he?

"Kattenttu!" yelled Kwian. "Curl up in a ball and rest! Become the sun and roll across the sky!"

Kattenttu curled into a ball of fire and became the smiling sun. He was free! He was no longer Kattenttu the Armpit, he was Koin the Sun! He rolled across the heavens, resting on blankets of puffy clouds. He nibbled Moon as a mid-nap snack. He smiled at the bright world of the San of the Kalahari: the hunters moving through the grass, the women singing as they gathered tsamma melons, and most of all, Kwian and the other children dancing in his sunshine.

PRONUNCIATION AND DEFINITION GUIDE:

The *Khoisan* language (language of the San) uses click sounds as some of its letters. *Kwian and the Lazy Sun* introduces two types of clicks, shown by the symbols | and ||. The clicks come before the pronunciation of the letter *k* in the following words: |kattenttu, ||koin, and ||kwian.

| is pronounced by flicking the tip of the tongue against the upper front teeth. When Americans scold someone they sometimes make this sound.

|| is pronounced by curling the tongue backward, resting its tip at the top of the back of the mouth, and forcefully flicking it down. This click is sometimes used by Americans to imitate the clip-clop sound of a horse's hooves.

See if you can say the words with the clicks!

|kattenttu (| KAT´ en TUH): Khoisan for underarm. Flick the tongue against the upper front teeth for the click sound. The *t* sounds are held for an extra moment.

||koin (|| KOI in): Khoisan for sun. Flick the tongue at the back of the mouth for the click sound.

||kwian (|| KWIH an): Name of a San girl. Flick the tongue at the back of the mouth for the click sound.

ttoi (TOI y): Khoisan for ostrich. The *t* sound is held for an extra moment.

tsamma (TSA ma): A desert melon and vine. The *m* sound is held for an extra moment.

tzenee (TZEH neh): A feathered stick thrown into the air and caught by another stick.

whai (WHAY e): Khoisan for springbok gazelle, a southern African antelope known for springing into the air when startled.